Through Rose Coloured Glasses

Through Rose Coloured Glasses

Racquel Helmers

Copyright © 2025 by Racquel Helmers
All rights reserved. No part of this book may be reproduced in any manner whatsoever without written permission except in the case of brief quotations embodied in critical articles and reviews.
First Printing, 2025
Without limiting the rights under copyright reserved above, no part of this publication may be reproduced, stored in or introduced into a database and retrieval system or transmitted in any form or any means (electronic, mechanical, photocopying, recording or otherwise) without the prior written permission of the owner of copyright.

First ebook edition: February 2025
First book edition: February 2025

http://rackers.co/

Original Illustrations by Racquel Helmers

Through Rose Coloured Glasses
Helmers, Racquel

There are not many things I would not trade to be able to speak to you again. There are not many things I would not do to be able to hear your laugh. There is only one thing I have been capable of doing to move through the loss, the grief, the emptiness. And that is to write. To write as if I were speaking to you, to write to fill the void, to write to get through to you. To write to get through to myself. To wade through the waves of grief that threaten to pull me under.

This book is to you, Mum.
May I forever look through the world with Rose coloured glasses.

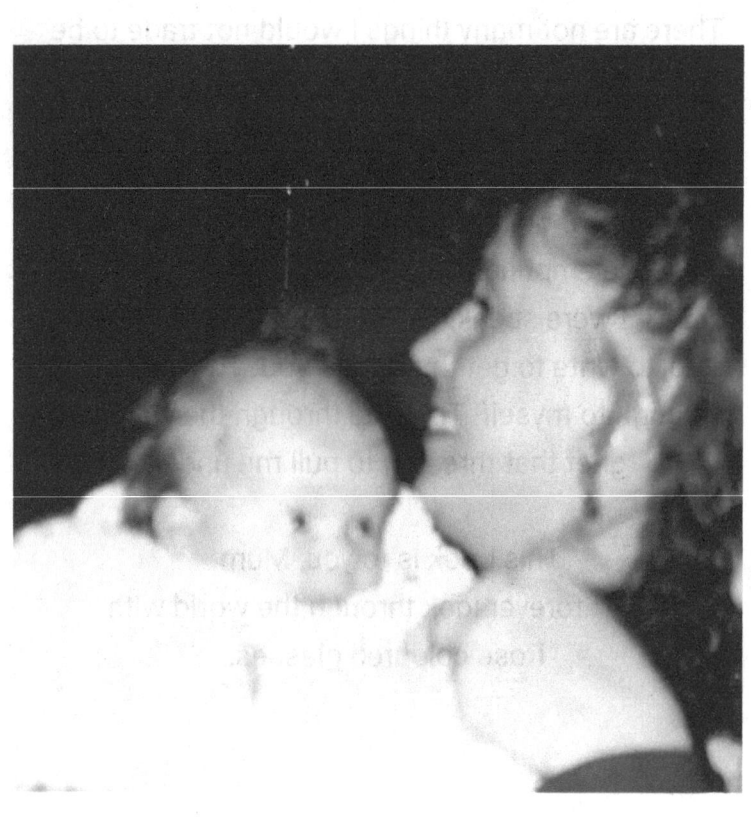

I am proud of who I am, who I've been, who I'm becoming.
I credit so much of that to you.

Foreword

The date of publication, 1st of February, is mum's birthday. How else to honour the years worth of birthdays that I'll live through where she is not here to celebrate? I began to see the world through rose coloured glasses when she passed. The perception of life transformed into something more precious, fragile. The hope that she would beat the cancer turned into a hope that I would exist; not only exist, but exist well. To do her justice. So with that: a collection of all my writings about mum, on grief, and the perseverance of hope through words.

4180 days.
Four thousand, one hundred, and eighty days.

It might seem nonsensical to go by days when you could simply say '11 and a half years'. More commonly rounded to whichever year is closer. This year, it will be 12 years; we're still closer to August. So 11 years. Within those 11 years was 4180 days to navigate without you.

It might seem nonsensical to go by days, but it is the most fitting way to get through grief. Wake up. Go through the motions. Go to sleep. Another day has passed. Wake up. Go through the motions. Go to sleep. Another day has come. Wake up. Laugh more. Go to sleep. Here we are again. Wake up. Crawl out of bed. Exist. Go to sleep. Again! Wake up. Smile. See people you love. Look forward to the next day. Go to sleep.

It might seem nonsensical to go by days, but it was more than a year and less than 18 months that I existed in a haze.

4180 days. It feels like an eternity and not nearly enough to capture the enormity of the loss.

The rain started to pour
as if the sky was feeling my pain together we cried
until I could no longer tell the difference between
my tears and the rain / my sadness and the earths
we mourned a soul lost to the stars
one less life blessing the day
one more light guiding the night

I had shaved my head mere months after you passed, raising more money than I could have ever imagined. It was still fresh, for all of us, so people were donating because *finally, something tangible I can do to help*. It was funny, to me, because you would have hated it. I had floated the suggestion months before you passed and you outwardly said no. You loved our hair. You taught us to take pride in our appearance. And here I was, without you to have a say, shaving it all off and letting it grow back all willy nilly.

I had met someone while I was out for drinks with friends, and he asked if I shaved my head for cancer research. Yes, I answered. He told me he had done the same for his mum not long before. I assumed, because here I thought I could relate to someone outside of my bubble, someone who would finally *get it...* I asked how long since his mum passed. He moved back, visibly awkward. *Oh... she's okay. She's in remission.* Oh! A mixture of shame for asking, and jealousy, and guilt on top of that. He didn't want to talk anymore. I said mine had passed months before. I wasn't one to shy from what I was feeling, even when I was young. You knew that. Why should I feel guilty that my mum had died? He outwardly said to me *I don't want to talk about this.*

I respected his wishes. I shrank further into my shell. *He doesn't get it. No one seems to get it.* But how could they not get it? How could they not understand that I had my world flipped upside down, and the only action I could think to take was to *shave my head?*

There were multiple times over the years I would go to speak about you and people would say they didn't want to talk about it. These were not moments of grief, they were human moments, they were natural conversation, but because the fear of death is so prevalent, I would say *my mum...* and they would close off. How dare the girl with trauma still speak of the dead? How dare she want to tell me about the best woman she's ever known?

Time has allowed me to accept people where they are. I will wear the grief, sometimes outwardly with a shaven head, sometimes inward, just on a weathered heart. I will wear it, because it is the least I could do. While you would have hated me shaving my head, Uncle Glen etched words forever carved into my heart. With his arms around my shoulders, and a rough kiss on the head, *you say she would have hated it, but there is nothing she would have loved more than this display of love and getting everyone together for a laugh and to cut your hair off. She would be so proud, kiddo.*

2014.

> **HAPPY FUCKING NEW YEAR. GOOD RIDDANCE TO THE WORST FUCKING YEAR OF MY LIFE. I'M NOT REALLY ONE TO BELIEVE THAT A NEW YEAR BRINGS GOOD BEGINNINGS, AS I KNOW YOU CAN CHANGE YOUR LIFE AT ANY GIVEN MOMENT, BUT THIS ONE FELT A BIT BETTER. NOTHING WORSE COULD HAPPEN TO THIS FAMILY, RIGHT?**

Happy Fucking New Year. I woke up on the second day of our 'fresh start' to my sister crying, trying to tell me something. I was still half groggy from sleep, only half able to decipher what she was saying; he's gone. He's gone. What in the world could have happened?

Do the rest of the family know? How do we tell them? Do we wait until they get to Sydney? Could we have changed something? We saw him just a week ago.

A week ago.

| 7 | - 2014.

How does that feel like a whole lifetime ago?

How are the boys? Are we going to see them?

Four months ago, we were in this place; people didn't know what to say to us, to comfort us, to console us. What do we even say now? Nothing sounds right.

I'm here for you — has since void of all meaning.

Happy Fucking New Year. The whole family's together again. We stand in a group, tearstained faces and all.

"Let's not meet like this again."

"Please, next time ensure it's a wedding."

May 8, 2016.

dearest mumma,

mother's day has rolled around once again, like we needed a day to tell you how much we love you. for you to know how much we love you.

today is our 989th day without you.

there are so many words i have tried to write. nothing... nothing works.

i miss you in everything i do. i think of you always.

for so long i felt like i couldn't live my life properly. i didn't want to live my life properly. how could i truly be happy if you were no longer around?
eventually, i realised how stupid this was.

do not ever feel guilty about being happy. that was all i ever asked for, all i will ever want.

| 9 | – MAY 8, 2016.

i lost a couple of good years to grief. one day i woke up and you popped into my head, *what the fuck are you so scared of? you're not the dead one ya dickhead. live your life for no one else but yourself.*

are you really not here anymore? is this not just a dream? some stupid, fucked up nightmare that i'll get to wake up from, in august 2013, and re-do life with you by my side?

my dearest mumma,

here is the deepest secret nobody knows
(here is the root of the root and the bud of the bud
and the sky of the sky of a tree called life; which grows
higher than the soul can hope or mind can hide)
and this is the wonder that's keeping the stars apart

i carry your heart (i carry it in my heart)

e.e. cummings

you da man roz.

I was grieving a whole life at the time all the people around me were starting to plan theirs. I was so far from ever thinking about marriage, the real career I wanted, having a family of my own. Suddenly, the reality that mum wouldn't be there through it all was handed to us on a dirty silver platter. It was year 12, and I was grieving a mum who wasn't even gone yet. I was grieving friendships of those who walked away rather than gave a shoulder to cry on, I was confused because I still cared about dumb *boys*.

I was never a huge future *planner* when I was young, but I was a dreamer. I had ideas, like we all do; I would get married one day, I thought I'd have a few kids, I was going to be a writer on the side of owning a cafe (and at one point, buying my own island...). I had a mum who was supportive but never unrealistic (although, perhaps her going along with my buying an island idea was a little unrealistic). She listened to my ideas and encouraged me in my pursuits, buying me my first camera when I said I wanted to be a photographer, to helping me decide the career path to choose in year 12. Would I have finished my studies as a teacher if she had still been around?

I started writing in my journal a couple of months after mum was gone; started as letters to her. I wanted to share with her what she was missing, I would relay situations and word it in a way that I would have told her. Over time, I learnt that writing it all down was for me. I needed to make sense of everything in my life, and I was used to talking it through with her. I started to craft it in a way that explained what I felt, rather than just relaying information. I could make sense of the heartbreak when I put it down on paper. I could feel better when I was complaining about something else in my life, because it reminded me that my life was continuing on, even without her. Life started to feel better a year on; more days were spent laughing, I was making new friends, and life had a semblance of normal. I was able to numb myself to how I was feeling because I would go to work, maybe go to uni, and then come home and sleep. Honestly, the entire year after mum passed away is a blur. I can sometimes pinpoint memories that fit in that timeframe, but when I think back to the time of 19-20, I cannot remember a

lot of it. I look back at the journal I kept, and I couldn't make sense of the things I was feeling; often, I wrote that everything in my head was a blur, that it felt like I was only having the same thoughts run through my head, and it was 'I am sad, I am lonely' and not much more than that.

I suddenly had to become so accustomed with goodbyes. Over the years, we lost more family members, pets, friends of the family. I watched those close to us have to learn their own ways of dealing with the ache, the confusion, to adapt to their new normal. I had faced so much loss, so much death, and yet I was consumed with heartache of the intricacies of my life. It began to get confusing when I was getting uncontrollably upset over mundane things. I could no longer separate how I was feeling from the grief that had pulled me under. What was the difference between reacting to the situation at hand, to piling all my issues onto one thing?

Trauma will nestle itself so neatly inside of you. Fitting so perfectly that, for a while, you may not notice it at all. An unconscious thing, not understanding why you feel so sick. The flicker of a memory, as if an old light in a dense, dark room. An unexplainable fear of mundane moments, things, people. The tremor of your hand that becomes second nature in uncomfortable settings.

We really understand our parents as their own people as we grow older. As we collect memories, experiences and we grow, the cracks begin to appear between a parent and just another adult; an imperfect human being. We all have these moments at different times in our lives; sometimes children learn it too early, sometimes adults learn it too late, and sometimes it's heartbreaking situations that make you face it. After these years, I have known but discover more that there won't be a time I don't miss her. Each exciting moment is coated with a heaviness because of the loss that will always be there. There are still so many days, hours, minutes of my life that I have yet to live, and each day I wake up knowing that not one of those moments gets to be in her presence again.

May 8, 2017.

> *Until it's gone*
> "Some people don't know what they have until it's gone."
>
> "But what about the ones who *do* know? The ones who never took a damn thing for granted? Who tried their hardest to hold on, yet could only look on helplessly while they lost the thing they loved the most.
>
> Isn't it so much worse for them?"

I have written and re-written the words I want to accompany this quote. It was the kind that hit me right in the heart, that resonated so much that I read it over and over again. The kind where you exclaim 'fuck' out loud because it rings so true.

I've lost count of the amount of times people have senselessly thrown the phrase toward those it doesn't apply to.

And I found the easiest way to try and get people to understand is to just read my feelings. No jokes, no poetic justice. Just words.

My mum was my best friend. I told her (almost) everything, so much so that my friends would tell me a secret and follow it with, 'don't tell anyone, even your mum.'

She knew when people hurt me and she could usually pinpoint who, without me even saying a word. She could see through my facade at 16 years old, when I had begun to think maybe I should keep my feelings away from home. (That lasted all of about 40 minutes after I got off the bus).

She was open about sex, bodies, love and life. She made me feel safe and so, so loved.

She managed to make all five of her children feel the exact same way.

I knew I was lucky to have my mum for as long as I can remember. I counted my lucky stars every day to have her by my side. I knew, *I know*, what I have and what I had was special.

I was five when she first battled cancer. Some of my earliest, and worst, memories come from the time she spent in hospital – the first time we'd truly been apart – I was in Kindergarten and I would cry at school because I just. Wanted. My mum. Maybe that memory was what created the bond that I don't have the words to explain.

I was 17 when she was diagnosed again. I still remember where every member of my family was standing in the living

– MAY 8, 2017.

room. Minutes before we had been laughing together. Seconds later we were holding each other, ugly crying our faces off, as if bringing our bodies closer together could fix it.

If love alone could have saved you, you never would have died.

For weeks, all I can remember thinking was 'why us?' And then, 'why her?'

Out of all the fucking people in this whole god-damned world. Why her?

I didn't know anyone less deserving.

She was a ray of light, a sparkle. One of those selfless, 'every day' people who made a difference in the lives of those who were lucky enough to meet her. With the most wicked sense of humour and one of those laughs that makes everyone happy to hear.

She was rare. And so beautiful.

She could make you laugh in your darkest moments, and was still making everyone else laugh in hers.

When she was diagnosed, my relationship with her didn't change. Because it didn't need to. I didn't need her to be sick to be able to cherish her. I already did that.

I would listen to people bitch about their parents and all I wanted to do was grab their heads and scream in their faces. YOU DON'T KNOW HOW LUCKY YOU ARE.

The week leading up to it was weird. Because I still knew what I had and how lucky I was to have it. Is this actually happening? Was all I would think. Surely she won't actually be taken from us? Wasn't it all just some cruel joke? But I can't do life without her! I can't! I don't know how and I don't want to!

Some people don't even encounter a love like that in one lifetime.

It was hard because that's when everyone else was coming out of the woodworks. The ones who that quote is made for. The ones who didn't know, or just simply took for granted, what they had in knowing a woman like her.

I was mad. I was so, so mad. I wanted to tell them all to fuck right off, to leave us alone. How dare you steal our last moments? We've known what we had all along!

I always knew what I had.
And I know exactly what I have.
Some may warrant my thoughts unfair, uncalled for, selfish, debatable.

17 – MAY 8, 2017.

But the thing is, the hardest pill to swallow – she didn't deserve to go so soon, because she didn't take life for granted. Life had thrown her curveballs that most of us couldn't even fathom dealing with, let alone living through. She deserved the long, happy, healthy life that so many do take for granted.

We knew that we had a best friend, the most beautiful woman in the world. But she still had her whole life to live. Children, in-laws, grandchildren. Fun, laughter, hope. She was still being taken. There wasn't one single fucking thing that we could do about it.

But I never took a fucking thing for granted, and she was taken away.
And that, some days, is the hardest reality to face.

You know, I think the crucial thing is that, while they're still around, you think *I could not survive without you.*

But you can, and you will.
And for a long time I kept thinking,
I'm still doing this because of you, and *I'm only coping because I need to, for you.*
One day it changed. I realised I was coping because I needed to, for me.

You had taught me as much as you were going to teach me while you were here, but I was only really learning from it while you were gone.

You had planted a seed of strength inside of me; it was just up to me to let it grow. So I did. And I still am. And I forever will be.

We are blessed when we find people, are bounded by and with people, create people – that give us a reason to keep going. A reason to live. Hoping you can be their reason, too.

There's a future version of me who is proud I was strong enough.

She looks an awful lot like you.

I'm not going to say to stop feeling sorry for yourself. I'm going to say to limit feeling sorry for yourself. I'll tell you to stop. Stop what you're doing and look out into the world. Watch every single person that walks past you.

Go to a coffee shop, sit by the bar with the glass window and look out at all the people running to catch a train. All the girls with one too many shopping bags. All the couples too in love to care. Then you'll see it — a bit of yourself — in everyone. And somehow, sitting alone in a coffee shop had never felt so good.

You can watch all these people and make up stories for each one. That woman in her business clothes who can run a little too well in heels, running after a taxi, running after her work, running from her mind. She throws herself into her work because she doesn't want to face what life is throwing at her. She's just hanging by a thread.

That little kid who's laughing with the old man, the old man watching in wonder at the pure innocence and happiness in his grandchild. You look a little closer at the man's face, whose heart is breaking at not being able to see his grandbaby grow up, the man whose been told he only has months to live.

The couple totally and completely in love. Still in their honeymoon phase, before they know everything about each other, before they've learnt the bad things; only the good. They have spent their past few weeks in isolation, getting lost in one another, slowly letting themselves fall for each other. Feeling things they had never felt before, feeling things they had blocked out for a long time. The girl only holding back a little, not quite letting her wall get broken down, because she's still hurt from her trust being broken last time.

The young woman with a brand new puppy, trying to replace a love she lost some time ago.

The man whose just lost his child, the child whose just lost their mum, the wife whose just lost her husband, the sisters who just put down their dog.

I'm all for crying, for feeling your feelings, for not blocking yourself out. But stop. Stare. Listen. And realise. You are not alone, and you do not suffer alone. Feel sorry for yourself. But not only yourself. You are not the only one struggling. You are not the only one who has lost a friend, a parent, a sibling, a pet.

Don't forget about your pain. But don't forget about other peoples pain, either.

You know when you cry so hard that your throat, eyes and head hurt? But most of all your heart. You rock back and forth, holding yourself, while you make that god-awful sobbing sound as you try to take a breath. You just know that you're pulling the ugliest face possible but you couldn't care less because all that's taking over your body is this heartache.

Do you believe in the afterlife? Can you?

I've had moments when I felt like those I've lost have been right beside me. Their signature smell wafts past, I hear their laugh, I hear their voice. Fleeting moments. I used to try to grab onto them, frantically searching for where the smell came from, which part of my mind their voice came from. But now I've just come to appreciate it when it comes around.

I have been asked if I could go back in time, would I? I've said multiple times that I'd trade anything to have mum back if only for a day. When I really thought about that question, I realised that I probably wouldn't go back in time. As much as it breaks my heart to think and admit out loud, I wouldn't.

I know I'd get so lost in my past that I would completely forget about my future.

I know you want some answers, but what is the right answer? There is no answer, just life. Just life.

One of the hardest things in life is accepting that it goes on. The world spins madly on. You wake up in the morning and it feels like the hardest thing you could ever do, to get up, get out and get on with it. You are so lost, and so confused, why is everyone still going on with their normal, day to day life? How? The world ended last night, so why is the sun shining again?

I wouldn't go back in time because it's not fair for the people who are with me now, to lose me to my past. I realise now that I don't need to go back and have my mum tell me she loves me, because all I need to do is look at what I have, and who I am. Every beat of my heart is a beat telling me that she loves me.

It's about accepting that there is afterlife for us, too, because we had to learn to live a life we had never lived before. With a hole in our heart we probably won't ever mend, but the ability to chuck a bandaid over it and keep on keepin on.

I just have to trust that, wherever they are, it's finally okay for them.

I'll obviously never know what comes after life, but I'll put my whole heart into believing that there's something more. That, right now, my mum has the calm, and happiness, that she always deserved. She's sitting on the couch in that beautiful, colourful, vibrant dress she left our world in, that perfectly matched her personality.

She's drinking a cup of tea and eating a block of chocolate and she's got her pups sitting around her for a piece (in this place, dogs are allowed to eat chocolate, obviously). She's with her sister, Karin, and her brother, Glen. After all the pain that the three of them endured in this lifetime, they are finally together again. Happy. Free.

It was winter.
Or was it summer?
I don't know; it was cold.
Whether it was cold
because it was winter, or cold
because my warmth had left me.
I don't know; it was cold.

My warmth.
The light of my life?
The light of my beginning,
perhaps.
Filled with happiness,
filled with strength.
Then it was gone.
Just gone.

Physically gone.
Unable to see; unable to hear.
She's somewhere though,
isn't she?
She's with me.

She's with me.

> You don't ever get over it.
>
> You don't ever get past it.
>
> You just get used to it.

You get used to the feeling of something missing in your soul. Waking up, and knowing there is someone who should be there, but isn't. Making a cup of tea, and no longer needing to make two. Making it exactly as she used to, because that is how she taught you to drink your tea.

You have someone else to call when you need someone to talk to. Even though it never feels right. Even though, four years on, you still feel like it's the wrong person to call. It is the wrong person to call.

You sit at home, on a Saturday night, and watch a movie with a tea in hand, a book in the other, because she taught you to always have a book handy. Always have a book handy.

'She'd like that,' you think, as you pick up a lovely long coat.

'I should buy that,' you think, because there's always that second that you forget they aren't around anymore.

Always that second that you forget they aren't around anymore.

You're in the shopping centre, you forgot it's almost Mothers Day. It's almost Mothers Day. Why does that day keep coming around, so fast? Another one. Another one without her.

Milestone, after milestone, after milestone.

They aren't there.

But they are. You know, wherever you go.

Somehow.

They are there.

You don't get over it.
You don't get past it.
You just get used to it.

I HATE YOU
I screamed
and the heartbreak
reverberated around the room.
I looked in my mother's eyes a woman I loved
more than everything
with each fibre of my being
I realised then
the impact of words
and the weight of lies.
I took her in my arms
as tears poured from our eyes
sorry would never be enough
It was the first time I held her
it was the first time I saw her
as more than a mother.
as a fragile human being.

You will have moments when you feel as if those you lost
are right beside you.
Their signature smell wafts past.
You hear their laugh. You hear their voice.
Fleeting moments.
You try to grab onto them, frantically searching,
for where the smell came from.
Which part of your mind their voice came from.
You learn to appreciate it when it comes around.
And let it go.

I've never been sure how to describe your being
whether you are
the sun, lighting the sky
the moon, guiding the night
or the stars
the most awe-inspiring sight

maybe you are all -
the trees, bristling in the wind the air, surrounding my skin

you are nothing
you are everything
you are every reminder
I am alive.

Missing you comes at random
when I'm falling into slumber
when I hear a song I know you'd like
when I see a stranger with your face shape
when I'm sitting alone in a café.
I don't know where you are or what you are.
You have become mere memories
but any moment I think of you
is a moment I am grateful.
I will never stop thinking of you because that way
you are never truly gone.

She will never die.
She may be physically gone,
but I will continue to talk about her, write about her,
think about her, laugh about her, and cry about her.

Our children will know about her, love her,
feel her in their very bones.
I will live for her.

I miss you more, and more, and more and more each day. I miss you in different ways. I miss you in my late night stupor, I miss you in my classes, I miss you when I look out the window and when I am driving home, or to work, or to grab a coffee. I don't feel pain so much anymore.

I am accustomed to this feeling, this small pang, this emptiness. I miss you, and I love you, but I am living for you. I will live and love with as much force as I can, for you. Because I miss you. Terribly. Inexplicably.

Wholly.

I dreamt of her
I dreamt that I wouldn't have her for long
so I was making the most of my time with her.
I woke up
with the thought of cherishing our time.
And I lost her all over again.

Have you ever missed someone
even before they were gone?
Have you ever thought
I miss them so
only to think
but they are still here?
Have you ever known it was the end
before the end even came?
Have you ever watched the end crashing down
like a heavy weight on your heart,
right in front of your eyes?
The fight. The battle. The stress.
And hard enough to admit, the relief.
There is no more pain.

But that is not true.
The pain never goes away
it seeps into different beings
disguised
a different pain.
A new pain.

You're missing something.
There's a piece of you that you just can't find anymore.
It feels like a vital organ has been
hastily removed
from your body.
You're just a little bit empty.
You become accustomed to the pain,
the heartache,
the tears at 2am.
The lost feeling when you awaken,
having just seen them
in your dream.
The moment you realise you can no longer
hear their laugh on demand.

I can tell you this –
Although they will never, *ever*, be replaced
your heart is big enough to fit more people in
if you will allow it.
Although you feel as if you are missing a vital organ
-- you are still breathing.

There was a moment. Long ago.
So much time has passed that I can say long ago and that is where my heart breaks again.

I woke from a dream in the middle of the night, lying on the couch with all the lights off. You stood above me, with your hand on my shoulder, you shook me awake and said, 'it's time to go to bed'. *You so disliked the nights I'd fall asleep on the couch and refuse bed.*

I mumbled my thanks, I kissed you on the cheek and bade you goodnight. In the morning, I woke in my bed.

I walked out and asked everyone who put me to bed, and they all shook their head. 'You refused so we turned the lights out and left you to sleep.' *My memory of you was so vivid. But it could not have been you.*

I spoke. I spoke of how you woke me up with your gentle touch, how you sent me to bed with your motherly love. They shrugged their shoulders or shook their heads. It was not them.

You had been here. For one more time. For the very last time. *You had been here.*

But does the fact that stars do not shine for lightyears away mean I cannot see you in the sky? I am convinced you are a star in the sky, but perhaps you cannot be seen. Perhaps, you will only be shown years from now. Your light with brighten the night, and a young girl will stare at the sky, with the weight of the world on her shoulders, and she will see you and she will feel light. She will feel okay. And you will be helping people you had not even met, and that is your legacy.

I dreamt of you for so often and in such vivid detail
that the moment I woke
from a night of restful sleep,
from a night of my mind
not even conjuring one image of you,
I lost you in an entirely new way
with an entirely new ache.

Sometimes the stitching on old wounds
come undone unexpectedly.
The pain feels fresh almost new
as if you had not healed at all.
And the process of healing
begins all over again.

The tears you shed
are watering the roots of your heart
the garden of your soul.
They do nothing more than allow you to blossom
for you are a garden amongst gardens
a flower
a tree
a sweet little leaf.
You are the nectar for bees
the sweet, sweet honey
you are the grass
and the earth.
Shed those tears
for they are the magic
to rebirth you.

Sometimes it's just a split second.
Seeing something I know she'd like
and the immediate thought
Oh, imagine how much she'd love that. I'll save it to show her.

(your mind is in some sort of default mode where life is where it was and isn't what it's been)

You realise, a heavy thud, a drop within the throat.
An accumulation of moments from the years without her
sit there in my mind,
tainted,
slightly crusted from the tears dried,
from the times before.
I file it away, sealed with the salty kiss
escaped from my eye.
Put it aside for the next lifetime.
Whenever we meet again.

The thin threads of grief woven
    artfully traced between them.

Linking in a way not achievable by anything else.

There is not much stronger than a grieving soul
than perhaps the love that got them there in the first place.

For we must always tread carefully.

One toe, then all five.

One heel, the weight of an entire leg.

Walking into a love that will engulf us until
life meets the after,
grief nestling itself in the corners.

You were called home
when it was time to turn
your scars into wings.

I think it is so beautifully fitting that her name
has to do with roses
because they not only smell like home
but they fill a garden
made like heaven.

I watch with an ominous envy.
   This was my favourite time of year.
Was.
The sun is shining, Summer is here.
The season of happiness. Laughter. Joy.
The stores are decked out with Christmas spirit.
Frazzled mums. Happy children.
Full of life. Love. Family.

I watch in envy.
That was us.
It breaks my heart that I want to skip the entire month of December.
A month full of promise.
All I can see is what I had.
Had.

Though it hurts – I fall in love.
With the gleeful giggle of the young child.
The endless wonder.
The time of year everyone comes together.
The reminder that: everything is okay.
And amongst the chaos, heartache and envy, there is magic.
Magic.

| 47 | –

You just have to look for it.

L ost.

For my 19th birthday, I was gifted a beautiful pair of Amethyst gold earrings. Naturally, I lost one of the pair one whole day after I was given them. I was devastated. I noticed it was lost at my brothers 18th party, so I literally began a search party at the party. We eventually gave up, and I've never found it again. My 19th birthday was my last one with mum. This was one of the last gifts I ever received from her.

It's been four years.

I still have the single earring sitting in my bathroom, a beacon of hope; hope that, someday, maybe the other one will turn up again.

During one of my sleeps on a Sunday, I dreamt of my Mumma. I don't recall what we had been doing, I just remember being in her presence. As I was in limbo between my dream world and the real world, I was saying goodbye as some tears fell out of my eyes. She pressed the earring into my hand, and told me she loved me.

"You found it!"

"I've always had the other one," she said, as she held her hand to her chest and showed me her necklace, made with the stone from the earring.

It's been four years.

Four years since I lost my earring, four years since I lost my mum.

I may never find the other half of the set, but I can always adapt what I have, to become something new. Something just as beautiful. Something just as special.

Said earring is now a gorgeous new necklace, resting on my chest.

August 23, 2017.

H^{ey ma.}

I was staring in the mirror before, searching for any piece of you that I could find. Whether I had your nose, your eyes, your smile. I stared for so long that my vision went blurry. I watched a tear trickle down my face and for a moment I hated that it was only my own, sad face staring back at me.

In the years since you left, I've become more emotional, wittier, weirder (if that's possible), stronger and more aware of who I am and what I'm here to be. In a way, I've become more like you. I think each of us, in turn, have stolen a piece of your personality and wrapped it in our hearts to guard for the rest of our lives. The moment we are all together is the moment you are truly with us, as if you never left; Kaarin's zest for life, Monique's quick wit, Caden's deep-seated love for his family, and Yvette, your little baby, her attitude most definitely comes from you.

1461 days.

— AUGUST 23, 2017.

Parts of you have begun to fade from my memory. I no longer wake up confused from a dream with you, thinking you are still here. I am used to it now. Sometimes that hurts the most. Painful memories plague my mind, like the moments I couldn't be what you needed. Words we should never have said to each other. Moments we took for granted.

There's so many things I wish I had have talked to you about, asked you about; guidance no one else can give but you.

I've never wanted to be defined by the loss of you. But it's hard not to be, when you are the reason I've come to be who I am. My proudest moments are when I'm told that I remind others of you.

35,064 hours.

The last words you spoke to me were in no way profound, inspirational, or in anyone else's eyes, the right words. All those nights sat up with just you and me and nothing else, with our hot chocolates and six marshmallows (each), are what I'll forever cherish most.
"Kel, can you make me a hot chocolate?" will always be the most important words.

Telling people you were my best friend doesn't do it enough justice. Trying to get people to understand the reason I am so all-encompassing when it comes to love and life, because of

AUGUST 23, 2017. - | 52 |

you, is near impossible. The reason I give it all or nothing is because I know what the right kind of love entails. You taught it to us and I search for it everywhere — sometimes in the wrong places, sometimes in the unexpected.

The most important thing the loss of you has taught me is the appreciation for life. Despite it all, despite the pain and the anguish and the shitty, shitty days — every day is a day I am glad to be alive. That laughing as loud and as awkward as I want, dancing like a giraffe on steroids, making people laugh and making people *feel*, will only enhance life.

2,103,840 minutes.

It's hard to comprehend that it's been four years since I spoke to you. Since I heard you laugh, since you held me in your arms. It's been four years of not being able to ask your advice, call you, just see you right there in front of me. You are but a memory, but my strongest, most prominent, most important, most loved.

"Kel, can you make me a hot chocolate?"

I feel almost a longing for what once was, or what should have been. There is a sense of belonging missing from me and I am trying to capture it from my past or create it within the confines of my mind.

Christmas day, 2012.

Our Christmases were the ones people wrote about, the ones they portrayed in movies and the ones people who "don't do Christmas" secretly envied. Sun shining, wine, beers, ciders and Kahlua & milk flowing, everyone on different jobs, walking past and reaching around each other in a sort of natural movement. Not a moment of silence, should it be the kids playing with their new toys or the adults telling a dirty joke, Michael Buble singing in the background or just simply the sound of happiness. Putting shit on each other, secretly feeding the dogs under the table and, typically, the tiff between siblings that was easily resolved by a dumb joke told by another family member.

It was our last Christmas together.

I remember a moment, where I looked around at the happy faces of the people I loved so much, the people I will adore until the very end of time, my people; and I let the distressing thought come in: *what if this is the last one altogether?*

I pushed the thought as far back as I could, refusing to believe it, though I think it made me appreciate that day even more than I would have.

Christmas was (and will be again) my favourite time of year. Mum had this particular magic about her all year round, but it was strongest in December. She thrived on the love we shared.

Christmas day, 2012.

I had just graduated school and I was beginning University in two months time. Life scared the shit out of me. I thought it would be the last Christmas where I was really, just a kid. I was right, but for all the wrong reasons. My biggest problem was a boy who didn't like me back and a friend who was flirting with me more so than usual. On that day, though, it didn't matter.

I had my people.

Whether I wouldn't solve things with this boy, whether I'd make silly decisions with the other one, whether I'd tank at university or whether I'd come to lose friends now that I wasn't to see them every day. It didn't matter.

I had my people.

Our next Christmas still had the magic, but it was a new kind of magic. It was a family bonding magic that we never had to deal with before. It was, hey, 2013 was a piece of fucking shit, but look at us all. Here. Together. Stronger than ever. And then we lost him, our ridiculously funny, inappropriate, favourite Uncle.

It hurts my heart that Christmas doesn't have the same magic anymore. It's a day I love with all my heart because I get to spend it with people who hold my heart in their hands, but it's not the same anymore, and it never will be.

| 57 | – CHRISTMAS DAY, 2012.

The magic of Christmas still sits in my heart. And I can feel it, pushing with all its might, ready to come out and sprinkle over everyone near me. Everyone I hold close.

Christmas day, 2012.
It is the fondest memory I have of my family to date. It is the magic that is sitting in my heart, it is the love I keep for those near and those up in the stars. I will never attempt to recreate it, but over time I will learn to make it magic in its own way.

It's the most wonderful time of the year.

55.

All I want to do when my mind is wandering off, off into 'fairy land' as you used to call it, I imagine and wish and want to hold you in my arms; daughter to mother, I want to hold you and reassure it will all be okay, everything will be okay, just like you had with me on so many different occasions throughout so many of the years you were here. Now I don't know if the person I envisage is you or if it is the part of me I lost when you were gone, I don't know if all I'm imagining is cuddling the child within myself ensuring her that we will be okay; that mum gave the little girl enough strength to see the adult through the years.

The grief hits at the most inconsequential times. It makes sense when life hurts a little harder and the pain of not having you feels a little stronger when I'm hurt by someone or things are a little more stressful, or big, exciting things are happening and you're not here at home to share them with at the end of a long day.

But then there's the moments out of the blue, when I'm driving home from the shops and my mind has been everywhere else or I'm happily singing along to my favourite song of the moment, and I catch a glimpse of the moon and I think of you, because I always think of you when I look at the night sky, and I'm crying, I'm blubbering and I'm a mess and I can hardly breathe.

Or I've been on holiday, aI'm feeling on top of the world and all of a sudden I'm under it, and I can't breathe as I watch the waves crash into the shore and I wonder where in the fuck you are and why I feel so alone.

Or, like this morning, when I'm sitting on the fucking toilet, and all of a sudden I get this rush of emotions and I'm crying and I'm rocking back and forth. While I'm on the goddamned toilet. So I'm simultaneously laughing and crying because I miss my fucking mother but, well, I'm on the fucking toilet.

When I'm disappointed by people in life, when people do things to hurt me or I feel as if no one is there, and it only intensifies the loss of you.

When it's been close to five years and you can barely yell in someone's face that the reason you feel so out of it is simply because you miss your mother. I just want my mum.

I don't even like my tea the way you used to make it for me, and sometimes that alone makes me hurt. There are days where I will make it exactly how we used to drink it, and I could swear that as I sit down with my cup of tea and the latest book I'm reading, I can taste your laughter and I can hear your happiness. Wherever you are.

I have lost what I considered my entire universe, but in a heartbreakingly satisfying way, even that is wrong. You were not my entire universe, because I am, and I know that you would be glad to finally hear me say that.

While you are, singlehandedly, one half of the reasons I am here, almost solely the reason I am who I am, and the strength that is pushing me ahead; I am learning, every day, that I am. I am. I am.

Because of you, but mostly, because of me.

I miss you, ma. I wish, more than anything, I was taking you out for breakfast for crepes with lemon and sugar and a pot of English breakfast tea, and we were laughing together and I was telling you about the things I find hard but in comparison aren't that hard at all; because that's a wonderland, it's a fairy land, that's in a different world that unfortunately you and I will never know. In this world, you're permanently frozen in time at 50 and you are memories, you are photographs and funny stories and a hot milo with six marshmallows, you are the perfume that I still search every store for to keep your smell. You were here, but you are not, and there is evidence of your life everywhere, everything shows you lived and loved but there are moments I can't remember your laugh or hearing you say 'I love you, kiddo.'

Because in this world, we don't get to sit together on your 55th birthday and toast to another 40 years of life together.

Instead, I retreat to my room, and I retreat to my words, and I attempt to put my entire heart on this empty page to give other people even a glimpse of what I am feeling. To hopefully give the people fighting similar battles the realisation that they are not alone, as much as I am not alone.

I miss you, and I thank you, for the years I had with you, for the years I have ahead of me, and most importantly, for leaving me with the most amazing family, as fucked up as we all are.

Here's to the first of February, the day the most wonderful woman in my world was born. Happy birthday, Mumma Rozza. I toast my tea to you.

Another Mother's Day.

Every time a special day rolls around, I debate with myself on whether I should write something for, and about, you. My mum.

It is the fifth mothers day without you, and the fifth year I still have so many words I could write about the love I have for you. Five years, and yet, five weeks ago I picked up my phone to call you. You would assume that after such a long time, moments like that wouldn't happen anymore; you would get used to the loss. I have, somewhat. In this particular moment, on this particular day, I forgot. I just simply forgot that you were not at home, with a cup of tea, cuddled up with the dogs. I went to call you, and I only realised I couldn't when I saw your name wasn't in my favourite contacts.

It simultaneously feels as if it's been a whole lifetime, and like it happened just last week. We had a friendship, a relationship, a love that could have put even Lorelai and Rory Gilmore to the test.

I'm coming so far in life, Ma, I'm becoming what I have always wanted to be and it feels so incredibly fucking unfair that you are not here. That you are not with me. You didn't even know I had this ability to write because I kept it hidden for so many years. I know, in the spiritual sense, you are with me. Sometimes, Ma, I just need you in the physical sense. I need you by my side, and I need you to call.

I'm tired. I'm tired of people blaming my mental health on grief, and sometimes it's the funniest feeling. All I want to do is vent to you, to tell you how stupid people are and how annoying I find them and how I want people to get that I struggle with mental health, and along with that, I miss you. I know you would understand, and I contradict myself in saying that maybe if you were here, if you could physically say to me you understand, I would be okay. But I don't know that, because I will never know a future life with you. I'm tired of people thinking they understand my mind, even when they read my writing; it's not even the slightest glimpse into what I feel.

I'm tired of people using you as their excuse. That they were "there for me," all that time ago, as if this gives them reason to pull me down; for me to stay the same, rather than become the person I am supposed to be. I was scared for so long of becoming who I am supposed to be because I thought that meant leaving you behind. Life isn't fair, and you made sure to teach me that. The loss of you instilled it in me.

Sometimes I can't conjure up specific memories of you and it throws me into a spiral of existentialism; it's life, you know, and just because you can't remember certain things doesn't mean you'll forget them (because, obviously, I'll never forget you), and I get that, I understand that, but I don't; why? Why did you have to go? Out of everyone? You?

Then there are moments when I get a jolt, and I hear your laugh, so crisp and perfect as if you are sitting right beside me, and I want to catch it in a small jar as if it's a butterfly and keep it; keep it to look at, to admire, to just simply have. But like the beauty of a butterfly, the memories are meant to fly by when I need it most; you are saying, "hey kiddo, don't forget I'm still here. I'm still here, honey."

What is there to say after five years?

You are still, you are always, the most incredible, most beautiful, best friend, best mum, best person I ever had the pleasure of knowing. And I miss you every goddamned day.

A note to all the lucky ones; who have a mum they care about, who have a mum who's still here. Please, for the love of fucking Christ, treasure her. Cherish her and show her how much you love her. Make her a cup of tea whenever she wants one and hug her, and tell her. Tell her how grateful you are to have her. Not just today, but every day. Because you may lose her next week, or you may lose her in twenty years, but when you lose her, there is no getting her back. All you are left with is, albeit a multitude of love and memories, inevitably an ache.

As you search for the perfect gift, remember that you are the best one they could ever ask for.

A note to the ones who understand where I'm coming from; remember the love she had for you, and share it with the ones you still have. Laugh, cry and live for her because she would want nothing less. You aren't alone in this, however much it feels like it sometimes, and as much as humans, and life, suck — it's so beautiful.

| 65 | - ANOTHER MOTHER'S DAY.

What's not beautiful about loving something so goddamned much that you hurt so hard when it's gone?

You'll have moments in life where everything is weighed down; not only your heart, your stomach and your shoulders and your head — when was the last time you were able to lift your head? When was the last time life didn't feel so heavy? You have to say goodbye to people who are *your people*; who aren't supposed to leave. Who are always supposed to be by your side.

And you're standing in a church, the walls so high and the room so ridiculously and unfairly come to be so familiar in the past five years, and tears stream so easily down your face as if it's second nature. Because it almost is.

Your heart breaks for your own family as you watch, yet again, everyone go through the same motions you've been through too many times before. Mere weeks later, your heart breaks again for a family you've known almost your entire life, for someone who was your first friend, for a woman who has lost the man who was her entire life.

But then you'll remember, and see. What they have made, the impact they have left, and the love the air is still filled with. Because of them. For them. With them. And while it feels like the darkest time, and you may feel as if nothing is worth it — honestly why should we even try anymore? What is the point in it at all? Give me a good reason to begin to bother with life again.

Think about the laughter. The times they made you feel so special, your heart was lighter than you ever thought it could be. Because they were angels amongst humans, and now they've rightly earned their wings. They are above you, always with you, always right by your side. The air on a crisp, cold day is their kisses, and the beauty of the blue sky is their smile. The stars amongst the night are them laughing with the ones they've finally been reunited with. And the sunshine, burning through your skin, is their reminder that your heart will feel light again. Never in the same way, never for the same reason; but in every way worth it. For them. With them. Because of them.

five years.

I don't know what to say anymore. It feels the same, and yet, I feel as if every word I have ever spoken or written about mum has not gotten near enough to what I have felt for the past five years.

You get used to it. And when you feel like there's something missing from inside of you, something that seems integral to the very soul of you, you're somehow still able to function without it. You're sobbing on the floor and pain waves its way through your body but the loss is no longer at the forefront of your mind; something new and fresh has replaced it and it seems nonsensical to be hurt by this new thing, but you are. This new hurt is just piled on top of the old hurt. Grief is just your old pal who's always around. Like a tattoo you never actually wanted in the first place.

It feels like a lifetime since I heard her laugh; simultaneously, it feels like I said goodbye only yesterday.

Another letter to my mum, because that's all I can do anymore. I can't pick up the phone, and I can't hear her voice. I can't kiss her goodnight and I can't ask her advice.

| 69 | – FIVE YEARS.

Ma,

It's been five whole years since I last saw your face, outside of a photo and outside of my mind. Five years since I looked into my favourite face in the world, the eyes that sparkle when they laughed and the smile that always made me feel safe.

I stood out in the rain before to let the raindrops remind me I'm alive. The raindrops mixed in with my tears and all I could smell was fresh earth and the beautiful smell of rain, and in a small moment, hot chocolates, while we watched movies on the Winter days I spent with you instead of at school.

In the past year, I have watched some of the closest people to me say goodbye to their family. All I want to do is hold them all and tell them it's going to be okay. Sometimes I'm not even okay, so I don't know if that's the truth anymore. All I know is that it reminds me of the day we said goodbye to you — the day I watched you take your last breath and any sense of the normal life I had before that moment, vanished. Completely gone. I felt as if I was out in the wilderness, and although I was surrounded by all those who I loved and loved me back, I was standing alone in a forest with no way out and no sense of direction.

I don't remember much of the first year without you. I felt lost and confused but I pushed that down and acted as if it were normal. I thought that was the way to do things. I thought pretending I was fine was the way to be fine. People tell you everything happens for a reason, and you're sitting there, smiling politely, nodding your head, clenching your fists out of sight because that single phrase could make you want to punch someone right in the nose. It doesn't matter if things do happen for a reason. For a long time, I didn't want to hear it.

Now, five years on, most days I forget that particular feeling. Getting the news you were sick. Spending my 18th birthday in a hospital by your side. Sitting in a chemo session with you instead of going to school. Laughing with other chemo patients and having people tell me they admired what I had with my mum. They admired that I was still able to make her laugh even though she was in such incredible pain. You never showed it. I never even understood it.

Sometimes, something reminds me. One of your favourite songs, or a new song I know you'd like. Your signature smell, or a woman in the shops with your dress sense. It's that feeling again. The feeling, when my heart dropped into my stomach, when I figured out you were really going to be leaving this world. We were sitting on the couch together, and tears sprung up in my eyes. I turned to you and I told you I love you. You wrapped your delicate hands in mine, and told me you love me, too.

The fact is, there is no such thing as a normal life. I know this, I've always known it – but I had what was close to one of the most blissful lives, filled with teenage stupidity and shitty friends. Everything was thrown into perspective that day, but even now, I still lose that perspective. I still get caught up in the stupid, shitty things people say or do; the confusion of love and life, and caring about things that don't matter. Perhaps that's a sign that life has gone as much back to normal as it can be.

What really matters in life if you're not doing your absolute best to make other people feel happy? Safe? There is nothing more I love than knowing the words I write make people feel something, or the stupid things I say make people laugh. I was put on this earth by you to touch people's lives and I thank whatever I should be thanking, every day, that I had as much time with you as I did.

You were, you are, the most beautiful, loving, all-encompassing woman I ever had the chance of knowing, of breathing the same air with, of sharing laughs with. Of crying on your shoulder and allowing you to cry on mine. Of being your own blood.

You were never given the chance you should have been given. To live a full, happy life and sometimes the anger I feel over that injustice shrouds my entire mind.

I loved you then, I love you now, I love you forever. Thank you for this life, Ma. I hope I do it enough justice for you.

alternate reality.

I woke up today and you were there. Didn't feel any different, it wasn't wrong, it was as it should be. You've been here for the past five years.

I walked out and you were sitting on the couch, slowly eating your weetbix.

"Morning Kel," as you laugh at my dishevelled hair and odd pyjama outfit.

"Morning ma," I say, walking straight towards the kettle. "Want one?"

"Yes please."

Two teas, white with two. I make it in our current favourite mugs of the time; they always change with the season.

"Would you judge me if I ate chocolate for breakfast?"

"Nah, chuck me one too," you reply, and I throw you a Picnic.

"Got uni today?"

"Yeah, but I think I'll skip it."

"Lazy ass."

I laugh, busying myself making the teas.

"Just feel like having a mum day."

"I won't complain, kiddo."

– ALTERNATE REALITY.

Mundane things, like helping you hang out the washing and updating you on my life. It had felt like I hadn't talked to you in years, but I swear I'd seen you yesterday. We drank multitudes of tea and took turns going to the toilet, laughing at our weak bladders. I made you crepes for lunch. We talked, and just talked. I told you how I'd been feeling and you held my face in your hands and you said it's all normal, kid. It's okay to feel this down, as long as you're working on it every day.

We watched our favourite movies and laughed and cried in the exact same spots. We napped at the same time of day, and I woke before you. I sat a moment, watching you sleep. The crevices of your face and the beautiful lines that showed a lifetime of hardship. A wonderful life. It was a melancholic moment, as if it was telling me something; your sleeping face, looking young, and peaceful.

You woke and I made yet another cup of tea.

"I'm having this weird sense in my tummy that something's a bit off," I say to her.

"Bit sad?"

"Nah. Different kind. Almost like this life isn't mine."

I looked over at her and a tear trickled down her face and childlike confusion ran through my mind. I held her hands in mine and I told her I loved her and she told me she loved me, too, and I had a sense of déjà vu.

Worlds colliding and in line with one another, an alternate reality. One I don't get to live in. A dream world.

January 1, 2019.

Looking back on a year feels weird and nostalgic and often a little empty. Where did it go? What in god's name did I fit into those 365 days? The most momentous times of the year jump into my head, like the highest of highs, where so much writing fell from my fingertips and I made connections with humans who understand me on a level I wouldn't have thought possible after knowing them for such a short amount of time. Seeing cities I have dreamt about since I was young and focusing all my energy on creating, making, turning the weird little thoughts I have into something other people can hold into their hands.

And, of course, the lows. A family so accustomed to good-byes, saying yet another one, two, three. Falling into moments of wondering what on earth it is all worth if this is what it all comes down to.

On the same wave, being able to bring myself out of those depths, a growth, a necessity; one I have taught myself throughout the year of what seems like nothing.

It felt like it went in the blink of an eye. What did I achieve? Wasn't it just 2017?

— JANUARY 1, 2019.

Learning the magic of trusting in the universe, the wonders of self-belief. And, being okay with having the most solitary year yet.

In it I stopped caring that I didn't feel like going out, that I didn't want to meet anyone new, that I wanted to focus on all that was going on in my head. In it, I became even more comfortable in being the person who sits here and pours out her entire soul on a little corner of the internet. In it, I began to understand my mum more than I ever had, leading me to feel closer to her after five and a half years without her.

And, today, bringing in a new year brings the memory of the ever-present, larger than life man we knew as our Uncle, my mum's brother, her protector. Five years since we said goodbye to him and it feels like just yesterday he told me to never stop being so fucking weird. Rarely seen without a long-neck in his hand, and always signing off the phone with an 'Alright, fuck off then.' Hoping to all that is the world, that in some way, somehow, the three siblings who all left this world too soon are together and rejoice in what those who are still here for them are making of themselves. Of the success, love and happiness they fostered into their family, whose very blood flows through their veins, and no matter how far they stray, they always know where home is. They always know who their people are.

Signing off from a tumultuous 2018, all I ask for in this new year is to grow with love. For those around me and those we've had to say goodbye to. And for those we may welcome into the family in the coming year.

56.

I started this morning with a Mumma Rozza breakfast; breakfast of champions. Chocolate and a cup of tea, for the day that should have been your 56th birthday.

Amidst the new year buzz and the phenomenon that is Marie Kondo, clearing out is always on the cards. Drawer after drawer I have emptied and now they all lay upon my floor... probably to go untouched until March.

I get lost in memories as I find old diaries, letters and birthday cards. How do you Kondo things that are virtually useless and just take up space, but the minute you hold them you are overloaded with memories of people who are no longer here?

Amongst it I find an old diary of things I wrote to mum for the months after she passed. It's easy to forget the feelings of old, and everything rushes back when seeing the handwritten musings of 19 year old heartbreak. I wrote to her as if she was right there, a conversation I wish I was having.

Everything seems so stupid compared to losing mum, it just feels so strange not being able to sit down and talk to her like usual. I feel like I didn't tell her how much I love her enough while she was here.

What I don't understand is how everyone can go back to their normal lives and expect me to, too.

I didn't know it was possible to feel this lost and alone with so many people surrounding me.

In almost every one, it's signed off with,

Can you come home now, ma?

I feel so far from that 19 year old girl who was trying to navigate everything in the worst moments of her life. Throwing all my energy into creativity and trying to make something out of the mess in my head, the mess in the world, the mess we are all living in.

I remember being plagued by dreams of you, and waking to only lose you again. Now you visit me in my dreams. I get to see you and laugh with you, and yet, I have this deep-seated understanding that when I wake, you won't be there. I am just lucky enough to see you in my dream world.

I miss the embrace of a mum's hug, one you can't find in anything else. Being able to come home, to call, to talk to someone who just gets everything you are feeling. Where in the hell would I be if you were still here?

How do you describe to someone new in your life, someone who was never lucky enough to meet her, that this feeling you carry around; these memories, this profound love, this something that exists in every corner of you, is because of the one magical person? How she was everything; hilarious, dark humoured, light in every way – home in a person, laughter in a cup of tea, comfort in one phone call. She was so fierce with her love for all of us and so passionate in the protection of her family.

Happy birthday to you, the most magnificent angel to ever grace the earth.

Easter Weekend, 2019.

A smaller gathering than we're used to, less people, less moving around. Even less food. Being able to fit on one normal sized dining table, rather than having to squish together and add extra bits to accompany all the family members. Of having a routine of being able to pass the potatoes, the broccoli, rather than everyone scrambling over each other to get their share.

It was the small moments of a family who have accustomed themselves to what they share and what they have lost, revelling in what we still have together. I stood in the kitchen to catch a breath after falling into a food coma and having to unbutton my jeans. As I stole a moment for myself, a burst of laughter rumbled from the room next door as another inside joke was pocketed for everyone for the future. A smile escaped from my lips as all I could feel was this incredible burst of positive energy surrounding people who had fought for a small amount of normalcy.

It was after, in the quiet moments, as everyone fell back into their own thoughts and their own food comas, sharing a bottle of wine and passing around a basket of chocolate.
I noticed smiles on each and every face, but most importantly,

EASTER WEEKEND, 2019.

contentment. A happiness in the moment and in their current lives. As — after years of suffering, as we have each had our issues to battle in the confines of our mind, as we have always come back to each other — it was a moment where everyone was at peace.

It was, as everyone had quietened down, that particular moment of silence after a large bout of laughter – as happiness settles down on everyone's shoulders – that I felt something else on my shoulder.

It was a hand, and a warmth on the side of my face as if it was a kiss. A whisper in my ear that said, "This is all I ever wanted."

Being able to see her children, all of them now adults; who over time, have only grown closer together. Who have fallen into step in their lives, side by side.

I wrote the words a while ago, *A family so accustomed to goodbyes*. As we said it yet again, to another person in our world; as we had to learn to restart, to shift what we considered our dynamics. To pause for a moment as it brought back feelings of old and learn to walk upside down on our already flipped world.

As the feeling of the hand passed, the warmth stayed with me. As we may have become a family accustomed to goodbyes, but we have become so perfectly gifted at hello's. At allowing new memories to join the old, as revelling in our old memories together as it only glues our bond stronger together.

As the laughter settles, and the happiness falls on each person's shoulder, she is there. Beside us all. Reminding us that the simplicity of us enjoying each other's company, of continuing in life together, is all she ever wanted.

It's the trickle of the warm tea down your throat. One you used to love so much, but you've lost the taste for it. But you still drink it, out of habit. You wandered so far into the forest of your own comfort, you lost the path to get out along the way.

It's not that the words have been sucked dry. It's that you run out of ways to craft the same sentiment. That living is exhausting and dying is fascinating and terrifying. That being in limbo, floating in the in-between, is somehow easier because it doesn't require much effort either way.

You wake up every day, because you're supposed to. The motions are always the same. Suddenly you're washing your face in front of the mirror and you can't even remember the steps it took to get you there. But you still do it, out of habit. You're not sure you even recognise the reflection looking back at you.

The kettle is boiling, you look down and you've already heaped sugar in your mug. You leave it in there, even though you don't really like having sugar in your tea anymore. Another old habit, dying hard.

The day moves slowly and quickly all at once. It feels sedate, yet you're surprised when you notice the sun setting on the horizon. The colours that blend within each other across the sky. You feel an inkling of appreciation, but not enough to soak it all in. So you walk back inside, and wrap your cardigan a little tighter around your chest. Close the curtains and flick the lamp on, leaving an ominous glow about the room. It used to feel romantic, but it lost its fervour along with everything else.

Time folds in on itself and you blend into the haze.

the Seventh Second Sunday in May

It's funny that every year, you forget what it feels like. The second Sunday of May is ingrained in my head as Mother's Day. It's something most of us remember from when we were young and made cards with shitty glitter and flimsy cardboard in school; but those were the cards our mum's would treasure. So, of course I always know the day is coming.

Every year, I wake up like any normal Sunday and I start to scroll through social media. Every second post and almost every single story is about mum's. Rightly so. You forget, every year, the pang you feel. That each year, these people get to celebrate their mum, get an updated photo to share, and get to tell them just how much they love them.

The thing is, over the years it feels like you should feel *used to it*. Knowing full well that you no longer get to make new memories with your mum, or do little things for her to remind her you love her. You grow older and know this day is hard for many people, from the ones who have lost their mum's like you, or those who have strained or absent relationships with their own. So you remind yourself you're not alone, but there's still pain when all you have is a memory.

It's the last drop of a discontinued perfume that I'll never use. I don't want to lose it. I soak in the smell when I need the comfort of her. It's the closest thing to remembering what she smelt like. It's a bottle I know I will keep with me forever and I'm terrified of the day it's gone. Whether I drop it and it smashes, the smell wafting into the air and escaping. If I have a partner who good-naturedly thinks he's throwing an old perfume bottle away, and you can't get mad at him because he was trying to be nice; likely not understanding that that's one of the few things you have left of her. Because you can have old clothes, photos & memories, but it's the smell that's distinct because that's one of the senses that goes first when losing someone. Maybe one day it will just get lost within moving boxes, or it will simply be misplaced and lost forever.

These are all hypothetical, but ones that wander through my head often, because I no longer get to make new memories with her. They are stuck where they were then, and even seven years on, it's hard to know that there won't be anymore. So I hold on to the ones I have; the clothes, the cards, the messages. The same photos because there will never be anymore; creating art out of those photos in a bid to relive and recreate the same memories we hold on to. The moments I think I hear her laugh in someone else, the nights she visits in my dreams.

She visits my dreams often, but she is always at an arm's length. My subconscious reminds me, every time, that she's no longer here so the dream is not real. Not allowing me to immerse in the feeling because I am trying to protect myself from being hurt when I wake up and remember. Time flows freely and suddenly you're years down the track, but she is still and always will be as young as she was the day she grew her wings. Always a distant but distinct memory. Always at an arm's length.

7 years.

Within 7 years, a child learns to walk, talk, converse, write their name & even start to read stories. They have memories that stick, they know who they are and who their parents are, what love is.

Within 7 years, a teenager grows into an adult; dealing with hormones, sex, experimenting and learning.

Within 7 years, you grow, recede, and grow some more. You learn and discover more of yourself, your values, your intrinsic self.

Within 7 years, every cell in your body is replaced by a new cell. Every cell who once knew her is gone.

Within 7 years, she had built her family and had her last baby on the way. She had two more 7 year cycles with us. The third cycle sees her baby turning 21 without her.

Within 7 years, I have become accustomed to a life without her and yet not used to it at all. I have thought of her every day, have cried out for her and only wished to be immersed in a mum hug.

Within 7 years, the weight of the words 'I miss mum' become heavier because they become lighter for everyone else. Time has passed, it's natural to miss her, but it's assumed the hurt isn't as present. You tell people it was 7 years ago so they think you're okay with it now; you're used to it now.

Within 7 years, you learn that some days the pain feels as fresh as it did on the day she passed. Other days it's just a distant beat of a broken heart.

Within 7 years, you discover that making constant mistakes is all part of the human experience and sometimes you will let in people who will only hurt you some more. Sometimes, it intensifies the hurt of losing her; others, it pales in comparison.

Within 7 years, you realise that perhaps, time doesn't heal all wounds. Patience and a desire to heal is the only remedy.

Within 7 years, you learn that grief nestles itself into you. It becomes a part of you, not your entirety, and sometimes it's so quiet that you don't even know it's there; nonetheless, a part of you.

Within 7 years, you adapt to a new normal but some moments, it still shocks you. You go to pick up the phone to call her, or you think of a question to ask; there's a sweet, blissful moment when you don't remember.

Within 7 years, you step more into who you are and find more pieces of yourself that reflect who she was. It makes you proud and breaks your heart all at once.

Within 7 years. Ma, I've thought of you every single day. I have felt comforted in the idea you're around somehow, somewhere. I have felt broken, not knowing how to get through to you or tap into the part of me that knew you. I have yelled into the abyss for taking you away. I have cried silent tears, and I have laughed when I remembered small, happy things about you. I have had days where I struggle to remember good moments, and those are the moments that hurt the most. But within 7 years, I have held on to the love from you and pushed through. I love you always.

If I could describe how I feel in a metaphor, it would be that I'm gliding along a corridor filled with mirrors; moving forward at a pace that I can't control. I genuinely can't tell if I'm moving forward, but it's assumed because that is how we speak of time. Sometimes I'm moving so fast that I can't recognise who it is that reflects along the corridor, it's all a blur. Sometimes it's so slow and I can only see a stranger back, but even she doesn't look like the person I thought she was. And then there are the times that I have a familiar face, the one I know to be mine, and I can stop and sit with myself in the mirror and find comfort with the person looking back at me.

Some days I don't know who I am or what I'm doing but I've perfected the art of pretending; the motions comes so naturally that there is another being inside of me that takes control of pouring the coffee, turning on the computer, even creating the art. Some days I will draw something and the next day I will be impressed with it, because it didn't feel like me who created it, and I surprise myself with my own talent.

I allow myself to swim in new ideas and immerse myself in the chaos of being inspired because I know the inspiration fairy doesn't always flap her wings near me. I work myself to the bone but sometimes burn out right before it's ready. So it, too, would move to the pile of almosts. The voice would creep back in, only quietly at first, and slowly it would get louder. It would push until it was loud enough that I couldn't ignore it.

Anytime I would even attempt picking something up from the pile of almosts, it felt as if I was physically blocked from doing so. I could only stare at it, often longingly, and somehow could never get started on it again.

I am in a limbo. It comes in waves; the times I feel completely content and as if I'm doing exactly what I should be doing – and the times it feels wrong, everything feels off and I can't for the life of me, remind myself why I do what I do.

It's someone else entirely who takes over my body when it has the desire to run away. It's never about dying, and it's barely about not wanting to exist anymore; it's not even about wanting to create a new existence. It's that this other being takes over and I want to push it away, and it so often feels as if the easiest answer would be non-existence. I am merely existing inside while this mask takes over.

I sat by the ocean and the feeling of immense... smallness washed over me. The vastness of the ocean and the entirety of the unknown made me feel both as if nothing matters, I am all but a miniscule blip on the face of the universe, but then also that the universe resides within me. The ocean is also indicative of emotions, and humanity, and all that comes with that. While nothing matters, everything does. All the world is, is a series of paradoxes. I could wade into the ocean and forget all that I ever have been as I allow myself to sink within its confines, or I could walk away from it and sink myself back into the mundane tasks of living. Would I be missed? Sure, for a time. But what is time? Is there a single moment where we disappear into the unknown? There is an invitation within the ocean just as there is into the unknown of afterlife. What is there to say of the lack of existence in the afterlife, just because we no longer exist on this realm? There is so much yet to be discovered within the ocean, some of which we may never know; can not that be said of life after?

Bringing me back from my reverie was the wind suddenly changing, adding a slight bite to it and the tinge of the sky faintly changed; indicating the end of the day was near. I do not know how long I had been sitting there. As I rose, I realised my decision was made for me. While the ocean was inviting, I would always walk back to land; not yet quite ready to discover what is waiting for me on the other side.

Alone seems like such a loaded word. The synonyms being; by oneself, on one's own, solo, lone, solitary, single, singly. And yet, out of those eight, alone is the one that feels just that: alone.

It sounds like the dead of the night, when all you can hear is your clock ticking by, each second passing you with each tick.

It looks like the one lone star, far from the brightness of the moon, with everything else covered by clouds & fog. The one lone star, twinkling down at you.

It feels like fresh, cold air seeping through your skin as you stand atop a mountain, surrounded only by hills, trees and the subtle push of the wind.

It tastes a little like tea right before it's too cold to even think about drinking; but it's still a comforting taste.

It smells like a waft of fresh flowers, slightly burnt toast and coffee made just how you like it.

It's remembering that being alone doesn't have to mean lonely, and each solitary experience cloaks you in a comfort of your own company like a blanket wrapped around your shoulders on a cold, Winter morning.

a letter to the youngest

There have been so many times and so many ways I have wanted to show you that I see you. I hear you. I feel you. I have wanted to say it and show it in ways that I'm not sure have ever made you understand, so I will do it the best way I know how: I will write it.

It's like when the doctor says depression is different for everyone, obviously; he said I was born with it, and yours was circumstantial. I have had moments when I am mad at the world for being born with it; why did I have to be born with the predisposition of everything being that little bit heavier? Where a default mode is a constant sadness? I was born with it, and I have to learn to live with it, but you had to live through something people should not have to at a young age. There are so many cruel things in this world and you had to be shown this when you were too young.

A weight was pulled over your eyes so everything from then on was just a little bit harder, heavier, tainted with an irrevocable sadness. You learned too early that life is just not so fair. There are two ways people can go when they deal with something like that when they are young; softer, kinder, and absorbent of the world around them, or harsh, cruel, and unforgiving. I am thankful in that you are the former; you still laugh through the breakdowns and fight through the bullshit.

Though we lost the same person, the five extra years I had were formative and valuable and you had to learn to pave your way in that I couldn't even imagine.

In this I want to show you that there is beauty in even the hardest of times. In the people surrounding you who are able to make you laugh just by one sentence, one movement, one weird little inside joke. In the days even rolling out of bed seems the hardest thing to do, it's another day toward a life of wonderful, shitty, beautiful things. And while you scream at the world for being so fucking unfair, for taking the best and most amazing woman we could have ever been graced with, all we can do is be thankful we had her, she had us, and we have one another. She lives on in you in the way you laugh and your sense of humour, and all you need to do is look at yourself in the mirror. You are more similar in ways you never have given a second thought to. She, the youngest; the world was harsh to her as soon as she came into it, but out of that mess she stepped out golden. She pushed on through, just like you. Look at the people around you.

Out of chaos comes a reverent beauty.

It's a cold night, considering how warm it has been. Cold enough for a cardigan, anyway. The water looks enticing. More than just for a late night swim. It's almost pitch black, except for the light on the boats out at sea, the light saying "hey, I'm here. Don't forget about me." I could do with some of that. The forgetting. Forget about me. Forget about everything. If I could just be erased. It would be quite easy, wouldn't it? To just erase myself. I find myself walking toward the water. It's warmer than I would have thought. The water laps at my ankles, almost like an excited dog. Notice me, notice me. The world means nothing, really. It wouldn't change much if I weren't here. If I just swam out to sea and let life do what it may. Life, or death. Depends how you look at it. Knee deep now. It would be so easy to sink in. You know those urges you get? That dark part of your mind. It's taking over. Throw your phone into the ocean. Jump off that ledge. Push that person over. You know the one you usually push to the back of your head, glad no one can read your mind? That one. My dress is in the water now, I'm waist deep. I forgot how heavy water made clothing. It's weighing me down but I'm not fighting it. I keep walking. Shoulder deep. What difference would it make? If I were gone. Just a simple footnote. They would grieve, and then they would move on. Simple. Life would continue with or without me. Everything is immersed except my head. All I would need is to let go. Walk a little further. Ignore my body's fight or flight. Just. Let go. It's all black now. It doesn't matter anymore. It never really did, did it? Life. Death. Depends how you look at it I suppose.

The wind is playing with my hair. The smell of the sea is strong. The smell of life. I'm standing on shore, completely dry. I haven't walked in. Only thought about it. Will continue to think about it, probably. All of us do. Some just have a darker counterpart. My light will always win. It always does. I give it the attention it deserves, see. Always will. I hope everyone else does. Give in to their light, rather than their dark. Nothing romantic about death, is there? Nothing romantic about grief. It holds on to you, once you've experienced it. It just, sticks. It's a part of your soul once death has touched your life in a profound way. I don't really believe that, you know. That I don't matter. That nothing matters. Of course it matters. That's why I'm still standing here, still dry. Waiting for the light. It'll come. Tomorrow morning. A new day, a new chance.

Give in to your light. Give it the attention it deserves. Your dark is strong, I know. But your light is stronger. You are stronger. I promise.

I have been waking up every day with a desire to live a life that is not my own; dressed in clothes that make me feel – and look – good, meeting new people, and sharing more laughter with those already close to my heart. Going on more adventures that extend the mundane. Exploring more than just the sublunary. Working towards something.

And yet, each day I wake and continue with the monotony. The same two-step slide, yet somehow expecting that to bring about change. I do not alter the current life I live to make way for the one I want. Regressing into the comfort of holding myself back; walking into an invisible barrier only created by the confines of my very own mind.

You can be full of hope and expectation, but you must keep about some of your wits; for the wits will tell you that the expectation without action is nothing more than fatuity. The hope will flake away and leave you only with despair for the life you never gave yourself the chance to live.

In the recognising comes about the knowing that yes, you can change if that is what you truly seek, and it only comes with the resounding efforts of your own. You can – and you don't have to – but to release the fear, you must walk through it.

February 23, 2021.

I have felt sad the past few days. An amalgamation of things, but my mind has wandered back to my grief. Sometimes it feels more comforting to settle into that sadness, because it makes more sense than anything else.

I truly thought I would be okay walking into a hospital, but the moment my foot stepped over the threshold, I was overcome. I felt heavy, extremely exhausted, and I wasn't even there for me. Memories flooded back to me from days in the hospital when I was 18, all the way back to when I was 6, always visiting mum.

I felt an ache at the idea of all my friends' mums now being older than my mum will ever get to be. I had a vivid dream with mum by my side, at 48, and she was sad because she only had two years left to live. I woke with a constricted throat and tears already dried on my cheek.

So today I will bask in it. I will allow the numbness to sit, the tears to flow. I will rest, I will write, and tomorrow I will get up again.

After these years, I have known but discover more that there won't be a time I don't miss her. I have seen and read from adults in their fifties who miss their parents. That I still have so much of my life to live, and so many milestones to reach, and each time it's an ache that she won't get to be here for them. Each exciting moment is coated with a heaviness because of the loss that will always be there. There are still so many days, hours, minutes of my life that I have yet to live, and each day I wake up knowing that not one of those moments gets to be in her presence again. It's the random days that hurt. While the birthdays, anniversaries and celebrations bring them to the forefront of your mind (as if they ever really leave), there are moments in a day you're going about your life when it feels as if someone stabbed you in the stomach. Only a week ago, I was sobbing into my pillow because I thought about the fact I will literally never speak to her again; I will never know a conversation further than the ones we had in her lifetime, and those memories have warped themselves into snippets.

The sound of the rain patters down, hitting the tiles on the roof and trickling onto the grass. The taste of tea lingers on my tongue from an earlier cup. I want to make another one, but the groove of my body against my pillows has curled into perfection. Faint rumbles of thunder in the distance and the sound of the monitor telling me my computer is still awake, waiting to get some work done. The breathy sighs of my sleepy dogs. The smell of a fresh book wafts past and it's the perfect soundtrack to a lazy Thursday afternoon. These still instances, a make up of a slow, quiet life. Moments of reflection. Of quiet contemplation.

It is the end of the day, and how much have I achieved today? Not much, to tell you the truth. I am in a period of simply existing. Not a period of transformation, not any growth; there is no romance, no bouts of inspiration, not even working particularly hard. I have indulged in leisure. I am reading more, sleeping more, moving my body when I desire.

Though, I am sitting blankly at the computer screen as words continue to deny their existence in my brain. I have an ache for writing, but there is purely fog in the part of my brain the stories come from. I have a desire to create many new things, but there is no drive behind the ideas. I write to understand myself, and all that comes out is a repetition; I am depleted.

I am in a period of simply existing. It is just about getting day to day, doing the work that needs to be done, but none spent on work I want to get done – a peril of the creative job is that you must (not really must, but it feels that way sometimes) be willing to create always.

There is something to be said of the days you can't get yourself out of bed. Not that they are good for you, but that they make you realise how capable you are on the days you fit so much life into one day. The bed ridden days are made for recalibrating, for letting your heart reload, for letting your body rest and your mind reset.

It is the end of the week, and how much have I achieved this week? Not much, to tell you the truth. I am in a period of simply existing.

There is something so heartbreaking and beautiful in watching your old dog becoming more dependent on you. Their own body starts to slow down and you are their guidance. Their eyes search for you in every room to know they are safe. They wait patiently by the side of the bed to be helped up because they can no longer jump. Their movement slows so they hobble along on your daily walk, still watching to make sure you are right by their side.

Twelve and a half years of love, gone in a split second. Their presence lingers and you will have to get used to not feeding them in the morning, not hearing their excited bark for food, not having them excitedly greet you when you walk in the door. It probably won't even feel real for the first few hours, days, maybe even weeks. This is something you learn is normal from all the loss you endure within your lifetime.

You will forget how much it hurts. Even after having dealt with grief many times in your life. Even if you're prepared, if you've known it's been coming for months, and it's your decision to help them go to sleep; you will ache, and it will be so confusing not having them asleep on your bed. Not having them follow you to the bathroom or react to a food wrapper. Not licking everything in sight, or hear their sleepy little sigh. Not hearing their snores in the middle of the night, or the pitter patter of their paws coming into your room.

You learn that this hurt becomes proof of a love so strong. That you may not have been able to explain why their body was shutting down, but they knew you were there by the gaze they would give you every day. By the need to follow you into every room to make sure you were still around. That while existing will hurt for a while, you were lucky enough for all those years you had the love that only a pet can give.

After many days spent unmoving in bed, anxiety attacks, depression episodes, he always knew how I was feeling. He would rest his head on my chest, or curl in a ball by my side, watch me from afar just to let me know he was there. He was my reason to keep going for so long. As he fell asleep forever, he held my gaze and in that, I knew that he knew he was safe.

over 3,000 days.

A random Tuesday night. It could be a Sunday, even a Thursday. It doesn't really matter anymore. There is a visceral reaction to a thought. To a single thought, and the thought is this: my mum isn't here and will never be here again.

Now, of course I know this. From the moment I am writing this, it has been 8 years, 6 months and two weeks. That is now over 3,000 days. So, I know this. I know it every day of my life now, and unfortunately it has become much more surreal thinking that she *was* here, rather than she *is not* here.

It just floated through my head. She is not here, and she will not be here. There is (presumably) more to my life, and each day, each moment, each exciting thing will not include her. Perhaps I will get married (perhaps I won't), she will not be here for that decision or for that day. She will not get to be a grandmother, and we all know she would have been the best of the best.

I often have these thoughts. Kind of a, *oh doesn't that suck*. There truly is not a day that goes by where she doesn't cross my mind. That, I have become accustomed to. What shocks me more now is when it hurts like it happened yesterday. People will always tell you that grief comes in waves; I have known this, yet you can't quite explain the feeling until you are in it. It hurt my whole body. I was angry. I wanted to yell at the world, but instead I just wallowed. I cried at the smallest thing in the TV show I was watching and it opened the floodgates. In a moment, I was sobbing and leaving tear-stains on my little pink pillow. I would calm. And it would come again.

A random Tuesday night. It could be a Sunday, even a Thursday. It doesn't really matter anymore. My mum isn't here and will never be here again.

Tears I didn't invite, but have pushed through the front door and I must welcome anyway.

I am imagining my 40 year old self meeting my 48 year old mum. A woman who doesn't yet know that her world is about to be flipped upside down and taken away from her. Seeing the young woman she raised who had to figure out her adult years all without the guidance of her mother. I am matured and the years show in my face but I trust that I am happy. I trust that in twelve years time, I have connected with the right people and perhaps created some of my own.

An immediate recognition in the eyes of both of us. Even if time travel has not existed, does not exist; if it happened, I know she would recognise my face in any timeline and in any form. I would take her for a cup of tea and crepes and talk about her life in a way that adults confide in each other; ask her the questions I never got to as a teenage daughter too worried about her own problems.

Alas. A dream, an idea, an imagination running away from the movie it was watching. Another world, another timeline, the same love. Always.

60.

The stark contrast of life and death and a life that continues.

Bawling my eyes out about my mum not being here for her 60th birthday, and within the tears, getting the text that our family friend has welcomed their new baby into the world. Elation mixed with sorrow.

The idea that I should have been at home taking mum out for dinner for her birthday, but instead I went to work and came home to an empty house, put Friends on in the background and laid on the couch for a few hours. It had become just another day.

I watch the movies and the shows that I know she loved when I need comfort, when I crave a mum hug, so I settle for a hot cup of tea, a cosy blanket, and the solace of these films. When I see a new movie I know mum would have liked, I make a mental note for the future; what for? I'm not entirely sure. Perhaps for the day I get to see her again. Perhaps to remember her even as I grow old; to connect with a fondness I have of her.

Writing a birthday note to the void because everyone will get to read it but the very person it's addressed to. Knowing she will never get to read the words I wrote to get through to her.

It becomes a distant longing, over time. No longer a surprise that there is a part of you that will ache, but almost a welcome part of you; there will always be something that will make you miss them, something that will remind you of them. Most times it is just something you deal with, but sometimes it's a wave of shock at how much it hurts.

The gift I bought you for your 50th birthday was a diamond ring that I now hold dear, tucked neatly away in my jewellery box, always reminding me of the one time I got to spoil you. I would spend my entire life saving to buy every diamond ring in the world if it meant another birthday with you.

As always, proud to be your daughter.

You don't look the way you used to. You see the extra weight, the wrinkles around your eyes, the trickle of age in your skin. So you take less photos.

You don't like the way you sound on a recording. You are critical of the inflictions, the nasally sounds, the way you pronounce words. So you don't take videos.

You shy away from the camera in the pretence that it's not needed.

I have no way of hearing my mum's voice anymore. I can't conjure it. I will get glimpses of her laugh in other peoples, but I will never know it again.

I have the same few photos to go through when I want to see her face. Much less from the ages I knew her best, from the beautiful face of the mum I remember.

I loved every wrinkle, the sound of her voice was home, the echo of her laughter was true joy. She cared how she looked, I just want to see her.

Take the photos, the videos, share the memories. Because one day they will be just that.

"Is this all there is?"

A rhetoric often spouted about a simple life.

A building dedicated to housing literature that passes through the hands of many — all reading the same stories, as the one book gets to travel through so many different lives. A day at the beach. On the verandah with a cup of tea. Waiting in the car on pick up duty.

A cup of coffee from the small business that trades on someone's dreams.

Buying trinkets made by the hand of a creative, sitting up at night by the light of a lamp in hopes someone will adorn themselves in their art.

The smell of the fresh, salty air and the sound of the crashing waves moving through me like medicine. Meditation.

The retirees spending their days by the beach. The couples having some time away. Young families soaking up the early days. People mirroring me, in every version that will come.

Is this all there is?

I hope so.

All I wanted was to call you. Not because I had forgotten I couldn't, but because you were the only one I wanted to talk to. The only one I felt I could pour all that I had into and you would make it – whatever 'it' we are searching for is – better, or just... okay. I had thought I had forgotten your number, which doesn't matter anyway because it belongs to someone new. Has belonged to someone new for almost ten years now. But I was falling asleep and the numbers just floated through my mind. As if every single thing I have ever known about you has just been sitting in the dark corners of my mind, waiting to be thought of again. Waiting on the other side, for you to answer.

I have uttered the words 'I want to go home' countless times over many years. Even while I was sitting in my home. I want to go home because home is being 10 years old in the house that dad built. It is the room in the middle of my two older sisters so I always knew I was safe. My night terrors would have me screaming my eldest sisters name in the middle of the night and she always came running. It is coming home with our border collie waiting at the bus stop for my brother and I. It is whispering to my youngest sister to ask for maccas because I knew mum would always say yes to her. It is waking up at 6am in the school holidays because there would be two hours of Lizzie McGuire to watch uninterrupted. This was home. I don't know if I'll ever truly be home again or if I'm just living in houses that pass the time.

ten years.

Hope.

The word, the thing, the feeling I so desperately wanted to hang on to that I permanently etched it into my skin.

The purple now so faded it looks like it could blend with the colours of my veins.

The posts become less and less, few and far between as time goes on because the ache begins to dull and there aren't so many words you can string together anymore; you have already said some iteration of them.

The pain used to feel sharp, as sharp as the tattoo, so the words would bleed as if a punctured wound. While the tattoo healed, the grief has not, but it's more of a dull ache now. I find it harder to put it to words.

I got the tattoo when I still thought there was hope that mum could live another ten years. That, by some miracle, she would be in remission for the second time in her life. Now I hold onto it as hope that things can always get better. That I can hope for peace, and healing, and love in different forms. Because as they say, what is grief, if not love persevering?

My mum taught me how to knit. I didn't really care about what knitting could do for me, but I liked the idea of sitting next to her with two cups of tea, something on the TV, while we knit away. I have since forgotten how to knit. If I learn again, it will be because I taught myself, not because she taught me. These little things that ache.

I have travelled, jumped careers, watched so many movies I know she would have loved. I have almost fallen in love, and I have walked away from someone for the most part because he never asked me about her. As if my grief was something to be uncomfortable about, rather than proof of the depth of love she instilled in me. I have been numb, I have loved loudly, I have remembered what is good and true and special about this life. All of this I have had to do without her. Without being able to call, to debrief, to just make her one cup of tea.

There are more people in my life now who never got to meet her, than there are who did. That number will only grow, while she stays as the most important to those who knew her, and only an anecdote for those who didn't.

Ten years since her scars turned into wings. Since I held her perfectly manicured hand, brushed back her fringe and got to say 'I love you' to her face for the very last time. Since I got to make that last hot chocolate.

It is the norm, and I don't know my life separately to this. Sometimes it feels like it makes the grey days even duller, but it makes the colours brighter. The smells even more fresh. It is now, instead, a comfort when I hear someone who laughs just like her. Smell a perfume she would have worn. Rewatch our favourite movies. To be told I remind people of her. To see my ageing face turn more into hers.

I am nearing the end of my twenties and I have had to do the entire decade without her. Where lucky people usually still have the safety if they need to fall back on it, knowing that there is a mum hug waiting for them when they need it. My early twenties were a confused haze of emotions, of blankness, of trying to be someone I wasn't because I was scared of being who I truly was without her. The constant battle of trying to tell myself I had it a lot better than others, instead of just accepting that it was okay that I wasn't okay. That profound love is a profound loss, and two things can be true at once: I was blessed to have her as my mum, and it was a tragedy she was taken young.

I wasn't given the time to understand who she truly was as a woman outside of being a parent, but these ten years have given me the time to understand who I am and what I want as a woman.

I'll see her again one day, but over the past ten years, I've learnt I see her every day. In my face, and in my siblings'. In the roses that bloom in places I didn't even plant them. In the wildflowers that grow out of bricks. The women who come into work, and have the same kindness in their eyes that she had. Our future families. The patience I have had to learn to give myself.

It is not the length of life, but the depth of life. You were a truly incredible woman. I will forever be proud to say I am your daughter. I hope to live a life as half as full of love as yours.

I can't wait to see you again one day, whether it's forty or sixty years from now. I know there will be a hot chocolate waiting, a mum hug, and a life full of stories to share.

The last time I saw my cat, I didn't know it would be the last time. I had taken her to the vet for a dental appointment and they called to say it was cancer. They asked if I would prefer to just let her go to sleep since she was already under, that it would be easier for her because she was in so much pain. I was faced with a heartbreaking decision, and I had about ten seconds to make it.

'Sure, okay, that might be better,' I said.

'I'm so sorry,' they said. 'We will call you and you can pick up the carrier with her ashes.'

Time passing feels like that moment. Like suddenly I have had to say goodbye, but I didn't actually get to say goodbye. I didn't know the last moment was the last moment. Time passes and it's two weeks later, and I have the carrier in my hand with her ashes in the other. The staff are gentle with me and honestly, I'm just... there. Like time is passing and I'm standing outside the window watching me hold it all.

I walked to the car and I paused for a moment because it felt so surreal. Wasn't it just last night she was curled up on my bed purring in her sleep? Didn't we just pick her up as a kitten a year ago?

I am on the phone to my best friend who lives on the other side of the world, but didn't we just finish school a year ago? Didn't we just celebrate our 25th birthday last month? Weren't we just sitting in a University cafe in our third week, excited by the prospect, laughing about the idea of getting on dating apps?

I have put the Christmas tree up for the third year in this cute little home at the coast. I am unsure if I will be in this house next Christmas, but wasn't it just my first week here? Didn't we just have Christmas with mum?

Time is passing as if I am merely watching from the window, like a montage of my life. I feel it, I am in it, but it is passing me by. The carrier still sits empty in my house.

Sometimes it's a spark, sometimes it's lightning.

Sometimes it's a little piece of dust floating through sunshine pouring in the window.

Over time, you'll learn to find it. To look for the light. To wonder where it's coming from next and how you'll come to find it.

Sometimes you will have a quiet thought, that it would be easier if you simply weren't here.

Sometimes it feels like you will never escape the weight that pulls you down.

Over time, you'll learn to know your worth on this earth. To talk yourself out of it. To know that your depth is a wondrous thing.

Sometimes you will be heaving through cries.

Over time, on that same day, you will watch the peach sunset and yell your current favourite song and know that your power is how deep you feel, so that makes the joy even sweeter.

glimmer of hope

It was a week or so after mum's funeral and one of her friends had offered up their holiday home for us. So the six of us, so fresh it felt confusing there weren't seven, went down to the coast for a week. We spent time together, we went to the beach on the cold September days, dad bought us fish and chips after fish and chips and we went for little walks around the sleepy coastal town in off-season and just simply enjoyed each others company.

It was the last day of the trip and we were walking down the street. We saw a pet shop. Caden, Yvette and I just said we wanted to have a quick look. There was only one dog left. We have never bought from pet shops before and I know I wouldn't again, but here was this fluffy little poodly looking thing. He made us smile bigger than we had in ages. At home, we had five dogs and two cats already. Dad said no more. We tried to walk out of the store and this puppy yapped and howled like I'd never heard before, as if he was telling us that we simply could not leave without him. Caden and I looked at each other conspiratorially; I had the money needed in my bank account. It was decided that we would split the cost between the siblings, and this sweet little dog would come home with us.

It's near 11 years later and I still have that sweet dog, who gives the best cuddles, who I wake up to curled in my arms every morning, and who is always beyond excited to see me when I get home. He was one of the first glimmers of hope I remember.

It is in the meeting of someone new. When you're content in the single life, it is easy to convince yourself you will never meet someone you will like again. You have the first, second, third dates and come to realise you like a person enough to want to see them again. It is in the excitement, the stolen glances, the hesitant touches as you begin to know them. It is in the shared laughter, beginning to bare yourself again, remembering how precious it is to show someone your vulnerabilities.

It doesn't necessarily have to work out, but the reminder that you *can* meet someone you like will spark the idea that, one day, you *will* meet someone who complements your lifestyle, because you just *did*. You have come to realise that the small romances have just as much sway and importance in your life as the lifelong ones.

The glimmer of hope is in the feeling. In the meeting new people, in the excitement. In parts of you being reawakened.

It is the day you spend in the hospital with your youngest sister. As you watch her and the partner she's chosen prepare for their lives to be utterly changed. It is the small touches, the care he shows for her, the making yourself useful while you wait. I walked into the room after she had finally come and there; that glimmer of hope. The tiny, puffy little baby resting on her mum's chest who has now completely changed my own world. I was the first person outside of her parents and hospital staff to hold her, and I knew then that I wanted to always be that person for her.

It is the life that is to come for her, and the desire to be around to watch it. To want to spoil her, and kiss her head, and smell her baby smell. It is the calm that comes over her as I sing to her, and the laughs that come out of her when Monique does her silly voices. It is the instant sleep when she lays in Kaarin's arms and listens to her tunes, and it is the first smile we ever saw her have in Caden's arms. It is the constantly boiling kettle as Yvette makes another cup of tea, the tv faintly playing in the background, the soundtrack of our childhoods now hers. It is watching her mold into motherhood as if it was made for her; just the same way it was for mum. It is the future and the idea that I will have plenty of nieces and nephews to spoil and dote over and be there for.

It is when I start to find myself again. When the incense is constantly burning, my journal is open on the table, the reading list for the year is hiking up in numbers. It is when I am cooking myself dinner, treating myself to lunches, allowing my body the rest when it needs it. It is when I write. And I have been writing. It is when my notes app becomes inundated with passing thoughts, burgeoning poetry, the floating parts of prose as I am trying to fall asleep. It is when I am thinking in prose again, when everything becomes material. It is the daily ritual of writing *something* so it can one day be *the thing*.

It is the glimmer of hope in each other, in my dogs, in myself. The minutiae of every day life, of the reasons to be here and the reminders of all that can be good.

There are little moments of care that people show you and you are reminded of the beauty that can be human nature. Your neighbours notice when you have gone away for another weekend, so they put your full bin out on the curb for you. Those same neighbours have noticed how much you hate to mow the lawn, so they mow the strip on their side of the driveway. You notice that the neighbours on the other side of you have started to do the same. You wonder if that is more in vanity of how your lawn looks in the street, but one comes out to you on a day your lawn mower is being temperamental and says to let him know if you need to borrow one. You realise it's simply care. It's the little waves you give each other as you're driving out and they are out the front. It's remembering each others' names even though your only similarity is the street name you share.

It's the patience as you show an old customer how to log in to her Afterpay so she can use it in store. Other customers wait, keeping themselves busy so as not to stress the older woman, until they can ask a question. It is getting compliments from the customers that had been around you, to commend you on your patience and care because, unfortunately, you don't see that every day in your customer service representatives. It is the fact that they didn't realise the care they were showing in their patience, too.

It is the phone call with your best friend as you openly share your delusions and the reminder that as much as you can feel alone, you never truly are. It is the daily messages from your sister because she knows you are struggling and her baby's face is the thing that brings you most joy. It is the family group chat sending stupid memes and whatever we know will make each other laugh, because we are constantly thinking of how we can continue to relate to each other.

It is in the self, as you allow yourself to cry while you feel down, unsure, lost. It is slowly moving off the couch and following your five step skin care routine, showing yourself the care even when you don't want to move. It is the endless cups of tea and washing the cup after every use so the dishes don't pile, knowing if they do you will feel overwhelmed and frustrated. It is caring for yourself in the moment to trickle into caring for yourself in the future.

becoming art

No matter what you're grieving, it always comes back to what you knew your life to be before and what life *'should have been'*. Growing up, you paint yourself a picture of what life seems to be for adults; often, you spend your time waiting for the day you can make your own decisions, do your own thing, be completely your own person. You imagine falling in love, building your own family, pursuing an amazing career, and/or travelling the world. You think every friend you have made in your young years will see you through to your adult ones.

As you grow older, you realise life won't pan out how you pictured. You learn to balance the beautiful with the heartbreaking. You go to weddings, and then funerals. You watch new life come into the world, and you sit by the bed of someone who is taking their last breath. You lose jobs, you get your heart broken, you choose to walk away from friends who no longer add something to your life. You discover you can't easily have children.

It's nuanced and complicated and entirely different for each individual person. There are worlds of ways to deal with the grief within life, whether that's losing yourself in your work,

BECOMING ART

reading to escape reality, running from your problems with exercise, creating art to express yourself.

Trauma will nestle itself so neatly inside of you. Fitting so perfectly that, for a while, you may not notice it at all. An unconscious thing, not understanding why you feel so sick. The flicker of a memory, as if an old light in a dense, dark room. An unexplainable fear of mundane moments, things, people. The tremor of your hand that becomes second nature in uncomfortable settings.

Life is generally all about going through the same sort of experiences but experiencing them differently. The one guarantee in life is death; the other being that you will likely experience the death of another before yourself. Art was the thing that truly forced me to feel. When I expressed myself for the sake of expressing, without judgement and with no plans on sharing it with other people, I began to heal. The words I wrote wove themselves back into myself and stitched up emotional wounds. The scars within myself became their own pieces of art, and everything about life became art, too.

> "ART enables us to find ourselves and lose ourselves at the same time.
> – Thomas Merton

'Twas the night before 30,
    and under the full moon,
the dogs were sleeping by the fire,
a new decade comes soon.
This decade of learning, of loving, of travel and growth,
a social butterfly and an antisocial hermit,
perfecting the art of both.
I learnt the little tells and how to trust my gut.
Settle? The dates I went through,
I made sure to do anything but.
I moved around and settled by the sea,
until my new favourite person was born
and my world changed by she.
It was the first decade without mum by my side,
but it taught me my own strength
and the love she left became an inner guide.
I found two careers that I love
as I go for yet another degree;
a writer, an artist and a counsellor,
I discovered I could do it all and still show up for me.
A spiritual girl, a lover, a friend.
I am in love with myself more than ever,
as my twenties come to an end.

There was a Tuesday at the end of autumn that everyone else thought was the same. For a few people, their lives changed. A new soul had joined their family. They were in a love bubble. They had brought another one into the world, and she was going to be weird. Quiet. Shy. Eventually personable, confident, and creative.

A Friday like any other. The footy was on, a night nearing the end of winter, the end of the week. For some, it was family members finally putting their issues aside to be together. It was a family sat around their matriarch, as she took her final breath. It was the worst day the girl who was born on the Tuesday had ever had to live through.

Wednesday in the middle of autumn, driving 600km to hug her little sister. The panic attacks had become frequent, the feeling of hopelessness ever-present. Her sister was struggling through her days, and they found the hope within each other.

A Thursday evening in the midst of winter, staying awake all through the night accompanied by instant coffee, cuddling dogs, and artworks to create a home to sell her art. Taking a leap of faith that would prove fruitful for self-development and confidence.

Monday in late summer, a cup of tea, unwashed hair and the first time feeling confident enough to sell writing. Knowing people wanted to invest in it, and joy overflowing from her fingertips right down to her soul.

A Saturday in the height of summer. Many people still revelling in their Christmas joy. Rostered on for the weekend, but the call came in at 3am and it was time to pile three dogs into the car and drive the 3 hours to the hospital. A new life. A new love bubble. A new personality to watch grow and shine.

Quiet Sunday. A comfort movie on in the background, a laptop laying by her side, her dogs curled up on her legs. 30 years after that particular Tuesday. Five days off her 11,000th day on earth. A life within days. Imagine what comes next Thursday. The favourite day that might overtake the Monday. The people to come, the days to love, the grief that follows, and the hope that floats despite.

How do you let go of things you no longer need when it was something they bought? Something that brought them joy?

A question that has been running through my mind constantly, lately. The first set of towels she bought me as a teenager: stained from all the hair dye, coarse from the many uses, starting to slowly tatter. This towel set followed me to each home I have had. I have bought beautiful new towel sets and yet, they take precedent.

The many, many pieces of costume jewellery that I will never wear, nor will my sisters. She loved to accessorise, how can I let go of these trinkets when she used them every day?

The books. The endless array of books because she was a reader and made us readers, too. So all the years of books we have added to the collection, only making it more than we can handle: I will never read all of them, some I am not even interested in. But how can I let go of books she wanted to read and never got to? The books she bought assuming she had more time.

The MUGS. She loved tea, hot chocolates, the occasional light coffee. Different drinks called for a different mug; it changes the taste... I swear. The countless collection of mugs filling the bottom drawer, stacked on top of each other, hastily shoved in to make room.

How do you let go of things you no longer need when it was something they bought? The things that made our house a home. The owl figurines. The candle holders. The cushions and blankets and vases upon vases of fake flowers.

It happens slowly. Books that would be more appreciated by another reader. Mugs to be donated for tea to be enjoyed in someone else's hands. The things that made our house a home, making someone else's house a home. It happens slowly. Trinkets don't mean they're still around. The everpresent thought of them does.

I still use my towel set.

O nce upon a time...

There was a big family who lived on enchanted land with all different types of wildlife. If you looked within the windows, you would see laughter, shared meals, and an abundance of love. This family had the most wonderful mother, who made each child feel special. The kitchen was always bustling with the smells of food, cupcake, the whistling of the kettle as another tea brewed. She was kind, incredibly funny, witty, loving and a little bit stubborn. Some would say she was magic.

One day, disaster struck. The mother passed on from this earth, and it left the family sad and a bit lost. But the remnants of her love stayed behind, and sprinkled on each of the members like fairy dust, so they always had a bit of her with them.

Many years later, while the mother was up in the stars creating different kinds of magic, she sprinkled down some luck with a bit of love. The youngest of the clan became pregnant. Within the same year, wedding bells rang, travellers were bound for the seas, and some were hearing the calling for home.

When she was born, the magic was created anew. The laughter was louder, collective effervescence abound. The love poured into every corner of their lives. And the mother smiled, knowing the soul she had sent down would bring the magic back, as each member remembered the story of ever after: they would be happy, and sad, and grieve, and laugh, and they would each know the depth of the beauty of human experience.

11 years between fridays

Friday, 23rd August. A really cold day. A crowded house, bated breath. A day expected but no less heartbreaking. Confused feelings, guilt for laughing. Family meetings. Anger and sadness and grief.

Friday, 23rd August. The sun shining, the air crisp. I spent the morning with my niece, as she cooed and laughed and bit my finger. I drove down the coast, the wind blowing through my hair, blasting and singing along to Signed, Sealed, Delivered by Stevie Wonder. The dogs slept soundly in the back of the car.

Eleven years have passed between these Fridays. Time and love and tears and laughs. The wound doesn't get smaller, but the love does get bigger. The capacity for letting more in. For knowing and being and loving good people. It started, but it didn't end with her. Love and laughter and life beyond grief.

It is in the quietest moments that things change: a sudden desire to be there, not here. Images of your future that float through your head look different to what they once were. A small decision with big impacts. A cup of hot chocolate, with a favourite show, three beautiful pups sleeping soundly. More phone calls with one of your oldest friends, ideas of planning trips to see one of your other ones, more time spent with your family. Writing, more often than ever; notes app filled with passing thoughts. Slipping out of the cocoon you had wrapped yourself in for a few years. The most content you have felt in a long time. Wrapped up nicely, like the end of a chapter is coming soon.

Crafting the same sentiment. All these words, all these poems, just to say I miss my mum. She created the family unit she always craved and it is cruel that she is not here to see how we have blossomed. To see the people we have become. To meet the ones we have chosen to build our lives with. To dote on her granddaughter. All these words, all these poems, to show she lives on. To know she lives on.

Acknowledgements

To my family.
I would be lost without you.

About the Author

I have told the story many times over the years, but Rackers Co started on a whim. Ever-evolving, Rackers Co started through a blog about life and dealing with grief, and slowly grew with me as a brand and a person. From learning, endless googling, dabbling in design for other people, Rackers Co is all about being creative – through digital illustration, handmade jewellery, artwork, and an online boutique. I have my Bachelor of Writing, Majoring in Creative Writing & Literature Studies, completed in 2019. From this stemmed the idea that maybe I could do something with my words. After dealing with a multitude of mental health issues over the years, I leaned into meditation to help calm my mind (also antidepressants). Over time, from the help of medical & mental health professionals, I have wanted to give back to others in the same way they did for me. I have a Certificate in Meditation Teaching, and I am currently studying my Master of Counselling. Care and understanding are of utmost importance when it comes to the courses and tools I create for you on the shop. As of 2022, I ventured even further out of my comfort zone and launched a second business & new home for my jewellery. It is now its very own brand, Solune Ave. Jewels, back under the umbrella of Rackers Co. Named after the sun & the moon, the golden hour as the sun sets and the moon has peaked out. It has been hard to navigate the million and one things and whether they should all stay within Rackers Co or whether I should make multiple businesses. At the time of writing this, in 2025, Tender Art Therapy has launched. I knew when I started studying counselling that I would have that separate from Rackers Co – connected, but separate. For a while, I feared that venturing on a new career path meant I was giving up on this one. Instead, I am learning how to let them coexist. I am not one single thing, so neither does my business need to be. To write, for me, is to breathe. So here's to many more years of writing.

www.ingramcontent.com/pod-product-compliance
Lightning Source LLC
Chambersburg PA
CBHW011522070526
44585CB00022B/2501